to: u   from: me

Alice White

BookLeaf Publishing
India | USA | UK

to: u   from: me © 2024 Alice White

All rights reserved.

No part of this publication may be reproduced, stored in a retrieval system, or transmitted, in any form or by any means, electronic, mechanical, photocopying, recording or otherwise, without the prior written permission of the presenters.

Alice White asserts the moral right to be identified as author of this work.

Presentation by *BookLeaf Publishing*

Web: www.bookleafpub.com

E-mail: info@bookleafpub.com

ISBN: 9789363305168

First edition 2024

DEDICATION

*this book is dedicated to: u tha reader from: me
tha writer . . . i hope u find what u are lookin'
for in tha pages of this book or tha next one . . .
& if u don't . . . keep searchin' til u do . . . never
give up . . . EVER . . . eVeR . . . ever . . .*

ACKNOWLEDGEMENT

i wanna acknowledge u . . . for being here . . . u
could be anywhere . . . but for some reason . . . u
chose to be here . . . with me . . . sooo thank u . . .

pspsps . . . i will also thank bookleaf publishing for
publishing this masterpiece for me & for u . . .

PREFACE

if u wanna know what it's about . . . read it . . .
tooo many secrets to go into here . . . u know . . .
& if u don't . . . u can fuck around & find out . . .

i wanna u . . .

i wanna listen to nirvana & hear u ask me how i
am
i wanna chill on my side & catch u up on all tha
fam
i wanna look out tha glass door & see tha trees
bowin' down
i wanna tell u i am good & feel tha peace in tha
air we found

i wanna push play & hear gavin say 'follow thru'
& me know i fkn did
i wanna show u how much alllll this means to
me, how much u mean to me & not be hid
i wanna tell u i made it home ok & everything
here is just like u said it would be (wish i
would've listened to u)
i wanna listen to u tell me things i don't know &
then hear u ask if ur intelligence insults me

i wanna be at tha lab with u & our scary movie
murda scene
i wanna feel u as close to me as u can get cuz
that's where we wanna be
i wanna go everywhere u wanna go & u take
care of me & me take care of u

i wanna touch u & be close enuf for u to touch
me, whenever u want to

i wanna taste u cuz, fkn YuM, u taste like candy
i wanna fuck u tooo cuz, y not? it'll be just fkn
dandy
i wanna let u have ur way with me, u know, it's
me u choke
i wanna roll US up into a joint & then it's US we
will smoke

i wanna laugh with u at stoopid shit & laugh we
will do
i wanna make u happy alllll ova again & have
alllll ur dreams come true
i wanna feel like this foreva & i know u do tooo
i wanna let u know our day will come & that ily

i wanna play trivial pursuit & watch u fill up ur
pie
i wanna watch tha clouds float by US & fill up
tha clear sky
i wanna be tha girl with most cake, i can be ur
HOLE whore
i wanna know u will be around takin' care of me
& US 4evamore

08162023

FU Boi . . .

don't wake up in tha morning & love me! it will
be tooo late
u have fkd this up for tha last time! ur love will
turn to hate
quicka than eva before, enjoy tha trip, don't
think of me
& i won't think of u, u will see, we will neva be

again, can't do this, won't do this, anymore,
who were we fkn kiddin' with 4evamore

my bombs were destructive but they didn't kill
tha wounded got up & started to feel
tha way i was feelin', then started to cry
whispered to me, 'i won't just roll ova & die'

'u know leavin' me is not what u want to do
but for some reason u think u got something to
prove
ur green eyes, ur sweetness, turn me to dust
havin' u around is an absolute must'

change has happened & attention is back
stronger than eva, just layin' out facts

where tha fuck have u been alllll day, when i
needed u mostest
who tha fuck knows but u def wasn't thinkin'
'bout me . . . the mostest
F U boi, ur trip, & ur mom
u will neva eva eva eva get from me . . . some!

u make it easy to answer without makin' a fuss
but also hard AF when u pop back up outta
nowhere talkin' 'bout 'Let US!'!

who tha fuck are u & who tha fuck am i
wastin' my time fkn 'round with this wtf guy
u know, i know, we both fkn know
we ain't here for no fkn show

sooooo STFU & speak now if u will
cuz it's really cummin' down on who to fkn kill

Heads or Tails BIOTCH!!!!!

08232023

stalkin' my inbox . . .

5

. . . u got me

stalkin' my inbox
& cussin' my outbox
to hell with tha roadblox
& keys that have no locks
tha clocks that go tictok
got thoughts goin' nonstop
tha tears that hit ur socks

are screamin' my name . . .

08312023

where's my mi.i.i.i.ind . . .

billie asks me 'where's my mi.i.i.i.ind'
but does she really have tha time
for me to dig way down & find
alllll that shit that's in a bind

my mind is high, where it is best
up up in tha clouds i must confess
cloud 9 is where, as a matter of fact
but i assure u, there is no lack

tha words tossed at me, tha adoration
far more than any imagination
tha speed & path that has been traveled
still draggin' ALLLLL that's been unraveled

what is this really, who is to say
& who will be there to stand in tha way
it was once said it could be called by no other
u know that word, it's like love~er

tha feel that is felt across tha skies
tha glance that is caught yet it passed thru tha
eyes
tha heart racin' fast & tha red in tha face
tha it's alllll movin' at such a fast pace

to one of them tho, a day's like a year
& with that, well, it brings a 'lil fear
tha other of them, sees a day like an hour
flyin' by so fast, there is no time to flower

tha two of them both pulled by tha connection
into each other with crashin' affection
like something u might see one day on tha big
screen
but def not like something that u have eva seen

how would one describe it in words used
other than fjipodWjpfiewTrjnjfoieFupi9eo to be
amused
but how would another understand tha above
if they have neva felt this kind of love

taylor's spent her HOLE life tryna put it into
words
but in this story there are just tooo many first
to list them out would be kinda fun
paper & pen, listin' them one by one

from a girl in tha lab to that HOLE whore
to openin' up ur HOLE heart & lettin' it allll
pour
from tha stars shootin' down right in front of us
to us both bein' in tha same room close enuf to
touch

we have our way & we understand it
& that's alllll that matters, IT's purrrfect
. . . we landed

09302023

stuck . . .

what do u do when u've been stuck
u have found urself in a rut

off tha rails, jumped tha track
tryna make decisions to neva look back

hard wayz, u know, do fall ahead
choices made, can put this to bed

left or right or heads or tails
tha answers lie in life's trails

tha love u had or tha one u desire
truth may be found in tha ash of tha fire

gotta look around if u're gonna see tha cage
& take another step to turn tha fkn page

goodbye to tha old, hello to tha new
steppin' my way a 'lil closer to u

what we have won't go astray
just cuz u tell me to go away

i'm still here but good i'm not

cryin' alllll my tears, smokin' alllll my pot

writin' this shit out so u know how i feel
cuz for some fkn reason, u think i'm not real

i will follow thru & then u will see
it is in love with me, u will still be

we'll get it together, our happily eva after
4evamore we will be & then we will die of
laughter

the end . . .

10032023

did u tell him . . .

did u tell him how u love me
did u tell him how we are
did u tell him how i told u from tha very start

did u tell him how our love speaks
did u tell him about our looks
did u tell him how every word we think is
written in tha books

did u tell him it's like tha movies
did u tell him it was fate
did u tell him it's about US & our late crime date

did u tell him it's indescribable
did u tell him it's 4evamore
did u tell him it is me that u fkn adore

did u tell him to go fuck off
did u tell him it's ur dick i sucked
did u tell him how we fkd & fkd & again fkn fkd

did u tell him how u're in my head
did u tell him how i'm stuck
i know u told him everything; NOW WE ARE
ALLLLL FKD !!! x3
10062023

wonderland . . .

are u wonderin' in wonderland
are u able to really understand

are u dreamin' of what could've been
are u wishin' to see me again

are u worryin' about it alllll
are u ova tha edge & now on tha fall

are u sad alllll day & alllll of tha night
are u mad cuz u thought IT felt sooo right

are u movin' on no matter what
are u thinkin' God, what a slut
   |onlyforuB^^^|

are u givin' up on alllll that was
are u givin' up just becuz

are u cryin' ova decisions made
are u drinkin' so tha feelin's fade

are u deservin' of alllll tha facts
are u ok or have u jumped tha tracks

are u gonna try to move along
are u gonna go ahead & play that song

are u forgettin' alllll that we had
are u thinkin' it was alllll bad

are u hatin' u for alllll of this
are u fakin' smiles for ur sis

are u listenin' to ur ramblin' thoughts
are u . . .
wait!
what?
are u what was lost?

FUCK! . . . i sure hope u're ok
with tha decision to just walk away
idk if there will eva come a day
that we'll both be ready & can just push play . . .

10152023.11042023.04172024

being fkn honest . . .

being honest ~ well that's a choice
some speak truth with their voice
tha some above includes not u
lies just spew out; what can u do?

being honest ~ well that takes guts
u are a liar, i am nuts
can't eva trust a word u say
am i able to write u away?

being honest ~ well that is raw
u are not that; minor flaw
truth can hurt, cuts down to tha bone
then u are left standin' alllll alone

being honest ~ that's ALLLLL i was
alllll trust in u, in US, just becuz
tha words u wrote masked ur lies
now i just cry bad byes

11122023

wtf are u | who tha fuck are U

wtf are U? & what have U done with me? what do U get out of tha love hate thing U have going? it doesn't look good! why? i just don't get it! & i don't hafta get it! but i would like to get it! how do U go from total i will do everything for U to we are done! it's extreme! U are extreme! U told me U were not a ghost. that is a lie! U are tha biggest ghost around! FU for making me feel like this! FU for thinkin' U had me! FU for fkn me up even more than i already was! FU FU FU!!!!!!

we talked about tha block thing! U don't give a fk! we talked about tha hate thing! U don't give a fk. maybe U are here to show me what it's like when others don't give a fk. idk but i sure wish i knew . . . this is a lot! It's alllll a lot! but it is what it is & if i have fkd this alllll up then i have fkd it alllll up! i will deal with it!!!

U are just full of lies . . . U are a liar! & a bold face liar at that!!! don't ya know?
yesssss tha fk U do!!!!!

U said you weren't a ghost! LIE

U said U would always want me! LIE
U said U loved me more than anybody! LIE
U said U didn't want to be tha bad guy! LIE
U said U would never hurt me! LIE
U said this was FATE! LIE
U said lots of things that have turned to LIES!!!

I don't wanna think about U anymore!
I don't wanna think about U anymore!!
I don't wanna think about U anymore!!!
GO THE FK AWAY!!!!!! LEAVE ME THA FK
ALONE!!!!!!

U can take U, & UR ghost & go tha fk
away!!!!!!!!! take it ALLLLL!!! i don't want
it!!! & U tell me i got problems . . . U should go
take a good long look in tha mirror!!! U got just
as many if not more problems than me
BITCH!!! i will see U in HELL!!!

i hope U got everything U wanted from me &
more cuz U won't eva fkn see me again or eva
fkn touch me again & if somehow someway we
can both end up lucky, U will lose tha key to my
soul!!!
i' will thank U lateR for opening up my eyes
BEFORE i fkd my life up even more!!!

08192024

u lied & lied & lied some more . . .

u came knockin' on my door
then lied & lied & lied some more

unsuspecting me, naive
said 'come on in, it's u i believe'

a 'lil shook but ready as never
ur turn to be ever so clever

keepin' my focus on u at alllll times
leavin' out details in alllll of ur rhymes

like 'i wrote this for my girl before
but i love u & not her anymore

i lie & scheme & make shit up
& with alllll that, i fill ur cup

to get to u, is what i want
& i always get what i want

every time, every chance
once we're here, u're in my trance

i can now do, what i want to
i will do it alllll for u

gatherin' up alllll of ur secrets
pryin' inside for alllll ur regrets

makin' a list & checkin' it twice
i will use it when u're not nice'

'tooo into me, being tha sweetest
i'll turn tha tables, kill tha fetus'

'i'm not a bad guy, just dress in disguise
u're learning lessons to make u much wise

tha lessons u learn, take them to heart
etch them in stone, don't eva part

i didn't love u, u were tha prize
i would never admit it, on that hill i will die'

12072023

she was clueless . . .

she was clueless, he was sus
she didn't know she couldn't trust

the words he spoke so fluently
flowed out his mouth like poetry

that hit came once, then once twice
it left her feelin' a bit surprised

she'd never felt like that before
he laid his heart at her door

she fell down hard, down she stayed
it was her options that she weighed

she chose him, what a mistake
he was a guy who was fkn fake

she wandered off into his land
got choked by his gentle hand

spoon fed his lies in little strands
just so she would see he's grand

revealed himself a time or deuce

she just could neva see tha red clues

was he tha man behind tha curtain
sooo full of shit & sooo uncertain

after days & days, reality sank in
she told him 'no contact' eva again

she likes to think he gives a fuck
she knows tha truth, he's lookin' for luck

he'll always be able to lure them in
yet, neva will they stay . . . it's just pretend

he's quick & smoooth & knows alllll tha moves
& is lookin' for his next girl to schmooooze

she knows now no way to not know
one day that fkr will reap what he sowed

he likes to think he's a Godly man
well God & his girls know he's a fkn scam!

ugghhh . . .

12092024

looks real fake . . .

when real looks fake & fake looks real
u can't be to careful, they'll come to steal
u from urself & u know tha deal
but u aren't u & new u likes this fake feel

u're still convinced it's u behind this wheel
driving ur fkd up life full speed ahead in this
make shift mobile
tha new fake deal u think is real; tha one that
grabs ya & has alllll tha appeal
keeps ur mind cravin' it as it is sooo surreal

but it's not real, u're not u, it's time to reveal
u're shown tha truth, alllll tha lies exposed &
unsealed
tha movie in ur mind playin' hidden truths
reel-to-reel
throwin' up, cryin' & u realizin' it was alllll fkn
fake, alllll unreal

realization to actualization MF; what a fkn
ordeal
u tricked me once or twice or
threehundredthirtythrice with ur real fake love
seal

u fkd with tha wrong one this time as i may be
lost but i am full of zeal
tha world will read alllll about u right here &
then maybe, just maybe, we can both begin to
heal . . .

12222023

mind obsessed

mind obsessed
she can't help it
thoughts possessed
she can't help it
no protest
she can't help it
fkn stressed
why can't she help it

tooo much was said
nothin' put to bed
no contact instead
deprived, face red

cryin' outside
dyin' inside
did we really even try?
why am i still here? why?

mind obsessed
she can't help it
thoughts possessed
she can't help it
no protest
she can't help it

fkn stressed
why can't she help it

it was fake real
with tooo much appeal
nowhere to heal
tooo fake to feel

oh but tha rush
hearts turned tooo flush
when words turned to touch
IT now yearned tooo much

mind obsessed
she can't help it
thoughts possessed
she can't help it
no protest
she can't help it
fkn stressed
why can't she help it

was it real fkn fake
was it a mere mistake
was it bound to break
why are u still eatin' my cake

is his mind still obsessed?

stuck in this phase
fifty plus days
mind in a maze
feelin's ablaze
thoughts in a craze
heart beats raise
lost in a gaze
comfy pj's
talkin' sideways
may hafta rephrase
cuz u neva know nowadays
neva saw US partin' ways

mind obsessed
she can't help it . . . & he can't either . . .

12222023

tha man u set out to sell me . .

.

tha man u set out to sell to me
is a man u'll neva fkn be
took way tooo long for me to see
it twas i who had been deceived
just like a kid, i believed
tha love we shared would neva leave
witch made it easy to perceive
oh what a tangled web we weave
talked about our life's philosophy
livin' it out togetha, responsibly
but that's not a part of this reality
hate it for US as i was ur eve
u once said 'u are bein' naive'
as u went on to steal my heart with ur key
little did i know, i'd pay tha fee
& then u'd get to fly away free

12242023

fkn fake fate . . .

ps sorry for tha fkn fake fate
u got in my head, i got in ur bed
psps thank u for tha late crime date

our IT vibe moved at a super high rate
without ever touchin' ilu was said
ps sorry for tha fkn fake fate

u would work tha setup, i'd take tha bait
chemically connected, we woke from tha dead
psps thank u for tha late crime date

together could we ever acclimate
what is tha chance u'll get outta my head
ps sorry for tha fkn fake fate

how is it that u make me ruminate
changed alllll my plans, now it's full speed
ahead
psps thank u for tha late crime date

u know it's our love that will devastate
tha people that love me might just drop dead
ps sorry for tha fkn fake fate
psps thank u for tha late crime date
12242023

FFS take 2 . . .

throw me 'round like a rag doll . . .
curl me up then touch me
slide ur fingers down my walls . . .
taste me . . . then u choke me . . .

don't feel stoopid, it's just us . . .
i feel stoopid, well i was
tell me how, don't make a fuss
why are we here? just becuz

wrap me up like a present
tape me down then drape me
u know we're both obsessant
rip me open then fuck me

don't feel stoopid, it's just us . . .
i feel stoopid, well i was
tell me how, don't make a fuss
why are we here? just becuz

who doused that water on our fire
we're done . . . go ahead . . . discard me
i didn't know u lost desire
alllll used up . . . don't touch me

don't feel stoopid, it's just us . . .
i feel stoopid, well i was
tell me how, don't make a fuss
why are we here? just becuz

don't leave me, thieves are waitin'
to snatch me up & take me
u love me, why u fakin'
heart's on ur sleeve, we can see

12312024

i'm not like me . . .

i'm not like me
how can that be
who is this she
that's so carefree
was it his tea
that made her flee
to find life's key
yet can she see
that bumblebee
buzz by tha tree
just wishin' he
was alllll she'd need
for her he'd bleed
neva concede
get killa weed
will she impede
or just proceed
heart, intercede
quicker than speed
done is tha deed
did it exceed
u sow, u reap
fkn black sheep
dug his HOLE deep
pretty damn steep

no one will sleep
he can now keep
his blah blah bleep

12312023

ur word . . .

'words are cheap', i told u a few times
yet ur words were what changed my mind

knew what to say, just what i needed
tha feelin's i felt, left me defeated

i was a mess, u sucked me right in
thinkin' one day, it was US that would win

as time ran by, ur words neva faded
i made a decision, one my fam hated

started steppin' ur way, let's give it a go
just to find out, alllll ur lies exposed

i needed to see u, so i asked permission
to drive up tha mountain, to talk, to listen

me on ur lap, safe, no alarm
u gave me 'ur word', sprinkled with charm

gotta start somewhere, so here's where we'll
start
'ur word' is alllll i eva asked for, i asked from
my heart

friday, saturday, now sunday high noon,
tha time for me to go is now, 'i'll see u sooon'

remember when i told u, 'words are fkn cheap'
wtf was i thinkin', 'ur word' u'd actually keep . . .

01212024

are u sure . . .

are u sure u don't want me to bother u anymore?
when i think that thought my heart drops, starts
to oooze, then to pour
it's fkn broken, smashed, pieces scattered alllll
ova tha floor
i start to pick them up as u sneak out tha
revolvin' back door

are u sure u don't want me anymore?
was tha plan we made not for 4evamore
remember? it's neva felt like this before!
& it is me & only me that u fkn adore?

are u sure u don't anymore?
u say it's me that u deplore
tired of alllll tha tug of war
endured alllll we can endure

are u sure anymore?
time is ova to explore
gonna stuff US in a drawer
wtf was it alllll for?
oh, u got to fuck tha whore?
& i thought we weren't keepin' score

are u sure?
no him, no her
we're; now were
no more recur
i don't concur
F U sir
blah, blah, blur

are u?

01232024

so u caught a mermaid . . .

so u caught a mermaid
then thru her back in
thinkin' she'd come back to u
again & again

what u didn't know
was that wasn't life's plan
thought u'd be good to her
& be her fkn man

she liked it alllll at first
the way u handled her tail
the way u supported her
the way u held her up without fail

but then came that tuesday eve
u cut her deep, wide open
threw her back in tha water
crossed ur fingers, started hopin'

she'd come back to u
like she always had
not knowin' alllll tha times before
she neva bled this bad

she's not comin' back, u know
u saw that water turn red
what u had with her u slayed
now nothin' more will be said . . . .

02082024

did dead done . . .

blank is tha mind
as i sit here in time
tryin' to write to rhyme
'bout u crossin' that line

it feels a 'lil sad
i know that's not bad
cuz what we once had
made our hearts feel glad

but now we're both crushed
ur skin is alllll flushed
yesterday we gushed
alllll seemed a 'lil rushed

it's alllll fkd up now
we both know how
just wanted to dow
life wouldn't allow

it twas real fun
'til u got out tha gun
u thought i would run
i didn't, so who won?

u DID this, i'm DEAD, we're DONE . . .

02082024

www.ingramcontent.com/pod-product-compliance
Lightning Source LLC
LaVergne TN
LVHW021314200726
843509LV00012B/1913